Is It Spring?

Written by Linda Ruggieri
Illustrated by Rick Brown

WR Weekly Reader Corporation
Inspire the future.™

Please visit our Web site at www.weeklyreader.com
For a free color catalog describing Weekly Reader Books, call 1-800-446-3355

Weekly Reader Books fax: 1-856-786-3360

Library of Congress Cataloging-in-Publication Data

Ruggieri, Linda
Is it Spring? by Linda Ruggieri
Illustrated by Rick Brown

Art direction and page layout: Tammy Gruenewald and Michele McLean
Contributing editor: Sue LaBella

Summary: A poem about some of the characteristics of spring

Includes bibliographical reference and index.

ISBN 0–8374-0008-2 (library binding)
ISBN 0–8374-0009-0 (softcover)

1. Seasons—Juvenile literature.   2. Spring—Juvenile literature
(1. Seasons. 2. Spring.)   I. Title.

This edition first published in 2003 by
Weekly Reader
200 First Stamford Place
PO Box 120023
Stamford, CT   06912—0023 USA
Copyright © 2003 by Weekly Reader Books

Printed in Brazil

Note to Educators and Parents:

Reading opens up a whole new world of knowledge, adventure, and excitement for children, yet we know that teaching a child to read can be challenging. Studies show that every child learns differently, so providing a variety of reading materials is important.

Weekly Reader, a premier leader in educational publishing, has developed a new picture-book collection called Weekly Reader Little Books, a series of Weekly Reader Books. Created by Weekly Reader editors, the collection is aimed at children aged 3 to 6 who are just learning to read. We have designed the books for teachers to use in the classroom or for parents to use at home.

Each themed set contains four books that are engaging, topical, and based on material covered in other Weekly Reader materials. The child-sized books feature colorful illustrations and simple text. Each book includes a glossary and activities that invite children to become active learners.

In the themed set Seasons, children will learn about various characteristics of each season.

Weekly Reader Little Books help teach children many important basic reading skills, including these:

• holding a book and turning pages • reading for information • identifying words using pictures as clues • reading from left to right and from top to bottom • recognizing letter sounds (phonological awareness) • reading words and sentences accurately and smoothly (fluency)

We hope you will introduce your beginning readers to the Weekly Reader Little Books and to the wonderful world of reading!
—Weekly Reader Editors

Words You Will Learn

budding: beginning to show buds

season: one of the four parts of the year—winter, summer, spring, or fall

spring: the time between winter and summer, when plants start to grow

Leaves are budding on the trees.

Each bird sings a tune.

Flowers are growing everywhere.

Will spring be here soon?

Children are playing in the park.

The rabbits and squirrels run.

**The season must be spring because
we are having so much fun!**

What Rhymes With Spring?

Which four pictures have names
that rhyme with **SPRING**?

Try This! Look on pages 5 to 10 to find
the six letters that spell the word **SPRING**.